The WAY to PLAY

ROBERT PACE

book 1

TRIPLETS AND TWINS

ON YOUR PIANO KEYBOARD, FIND THE TRIPLETS (THREE BLACK KEYS)

NEXT, FIND A SET OF TWINS (TWO BLACK KEYS) AND PLAY THEM.

GO UP THE KEYBOARD ON THE TRIPLETS AND COME BACK DOWN ON THE TWINS. TRY THIS SEVERAL TIMES.

FIND THE HIGHEST TRIPLETS-THEN THOSE IN THE MIDDLE - AND FINALLY, THOSE DOWN LOW.

CAN YOU FIND THE LOWEST TWINS AND THEN GO TO THE TOP?

NOW, WITHOUT LOOKING AT THE KEYBOARD, FIND TRIPLETS AND TWINS HIGH AND LOW. WHEN YOU THINK YOU HAVE FOUND THEM, LOOK TO SEE IF YOU ARE CORRECT.

HAVE FUN WITH THIS A FEW MINUTES EACH DAY AT HOME.

FINGER WIGGLERS

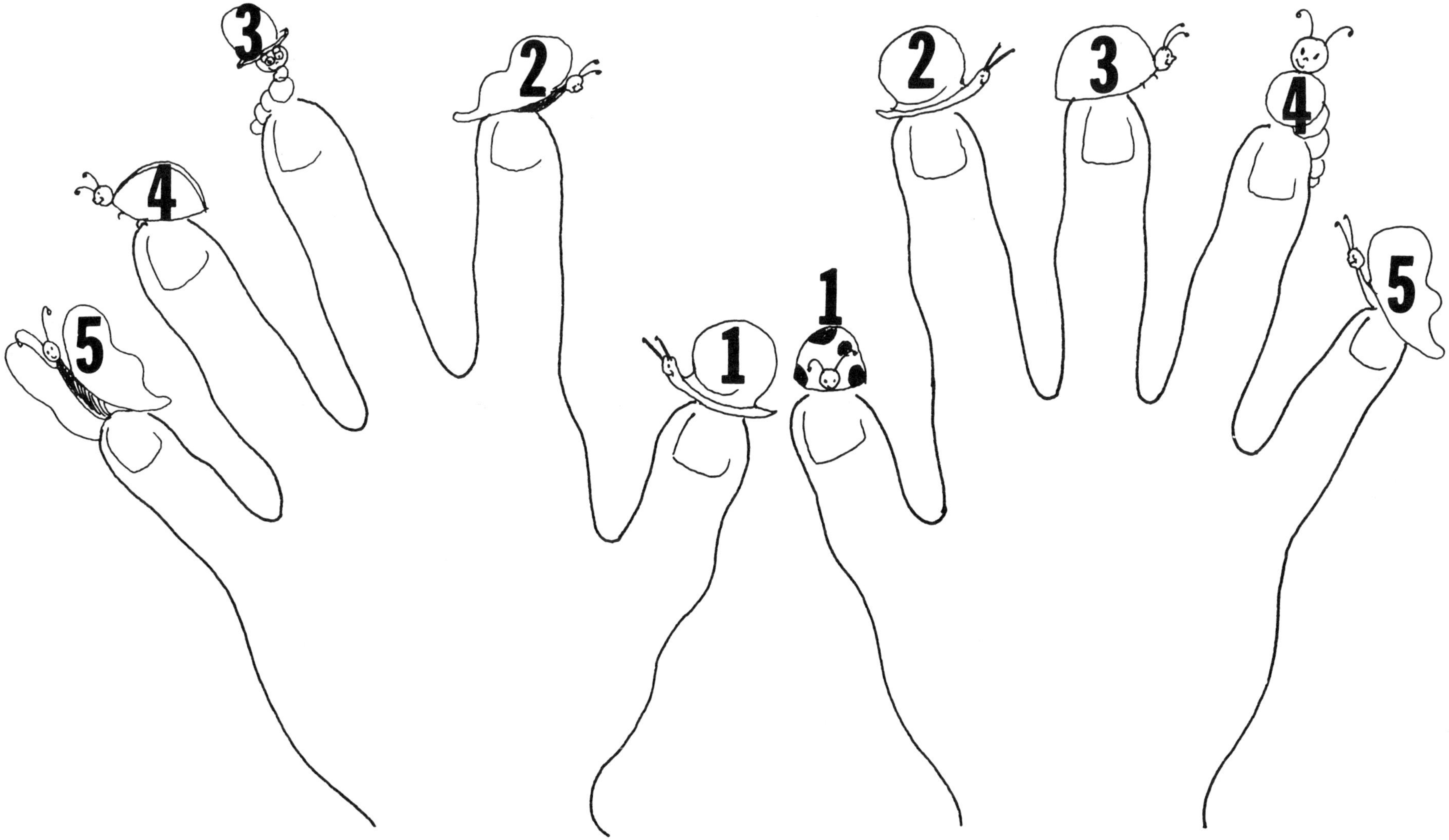

LET'S NUMBER OUR FINGERS:

WIGGLE THE ONES WIGGLE THE TWOS WIGGLE THE THREES WIGGLE THE FOURS WIGGLE THE FIVES

NOW WIGGLE ONE, AND TWO AND THREE - THEN THREE AND TWO AND ONE.

NEXT, MAKE UP FINGER WIGGLERS OF YOUR OWN, AND DON'T LOOK AT YOUR HANDS.

STEPPING

1. Sing the finger numbers as you shape this melody in the air.
2. Sing again as you clap the rhythm.
3. Sing the finger numbers again, but this time pretend you are playing it in the air. Move each finger as you sing its number.
4. Now sing it as you play it on the piano.

Right Hand

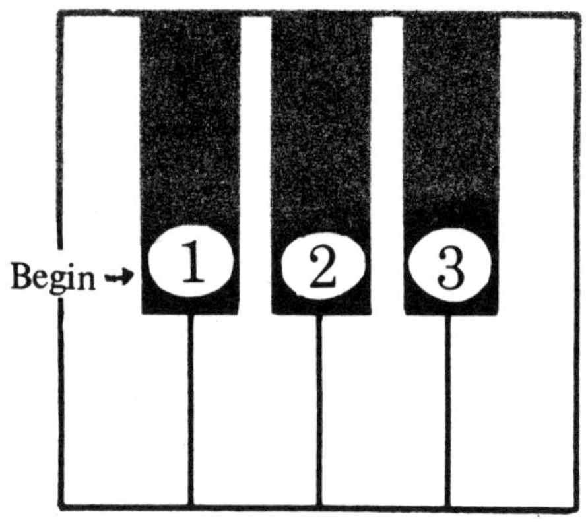

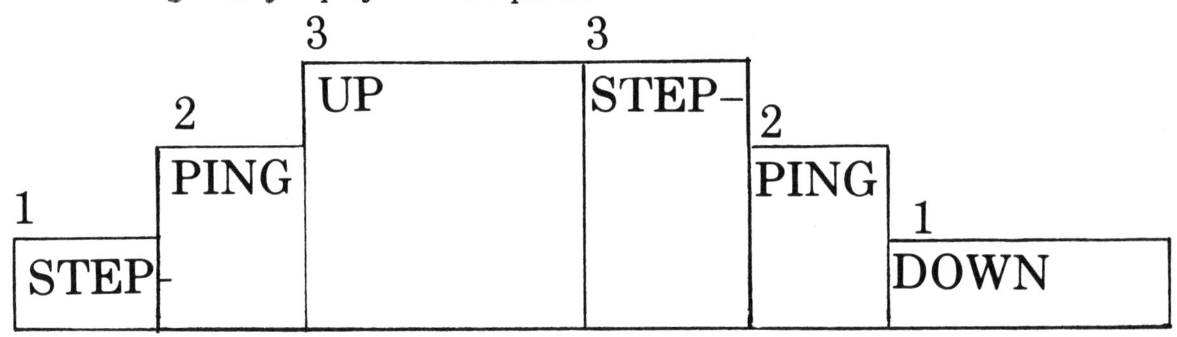

Left Hand

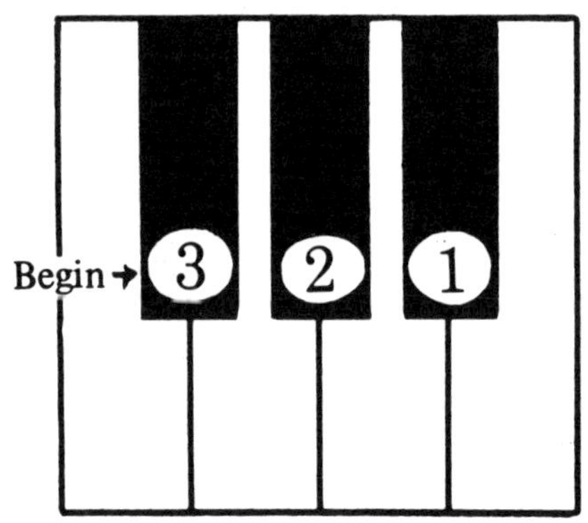

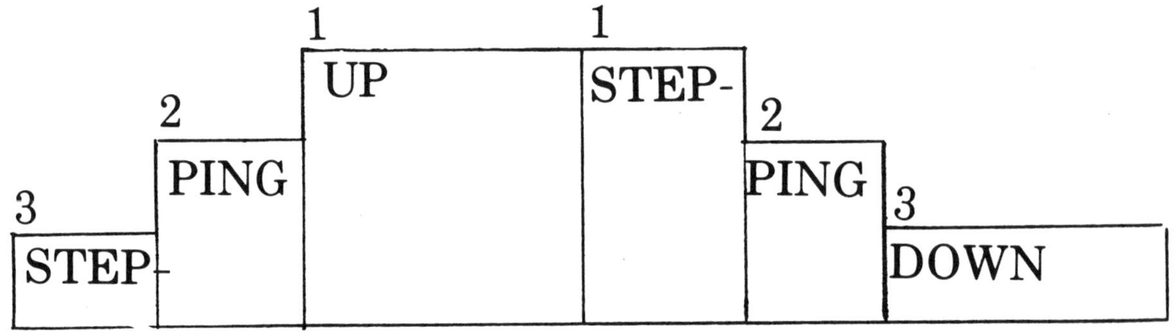

Find the three white keys just to the right of the triplets and play this again. This is called *transposing*.

If you move each finger one white note to the left, you have another place to play it.

Right Hand

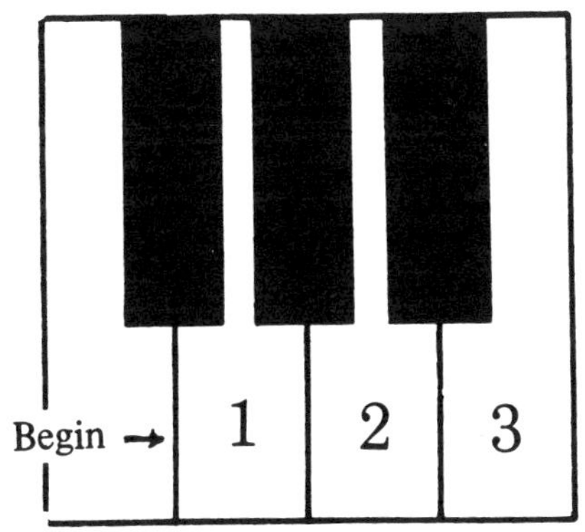

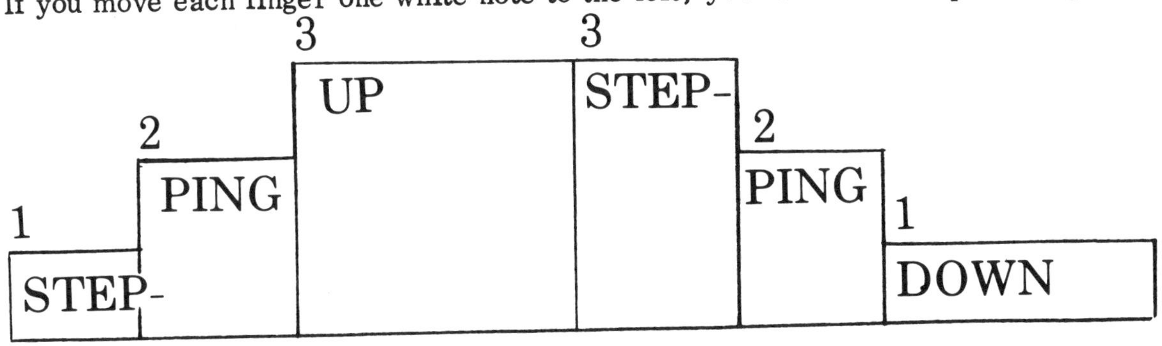

Left Hand

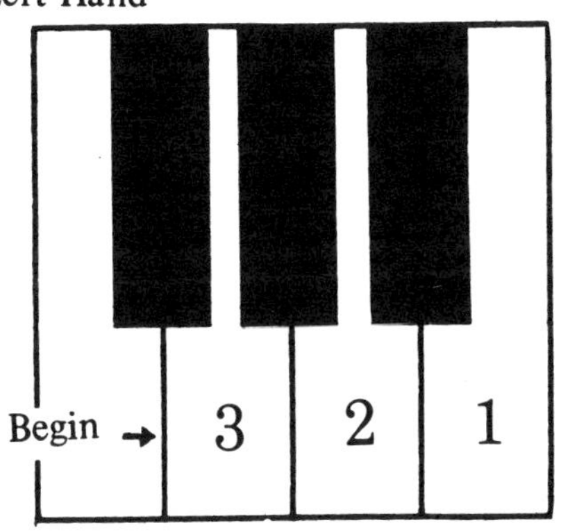

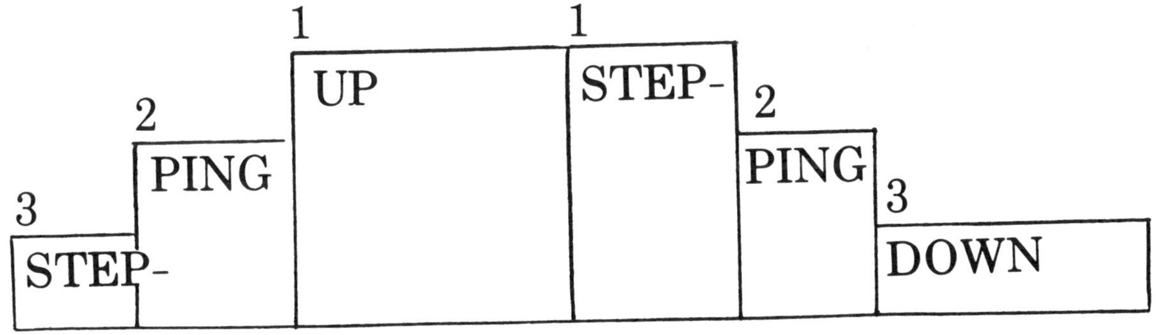

HOT CROSS BUNS

1. Sing and shape the melody.
2. Sing and clap the rhythm.
3. Sing and play the melody in the air.
4. Sing and play the melody on the piano.

Right Hand

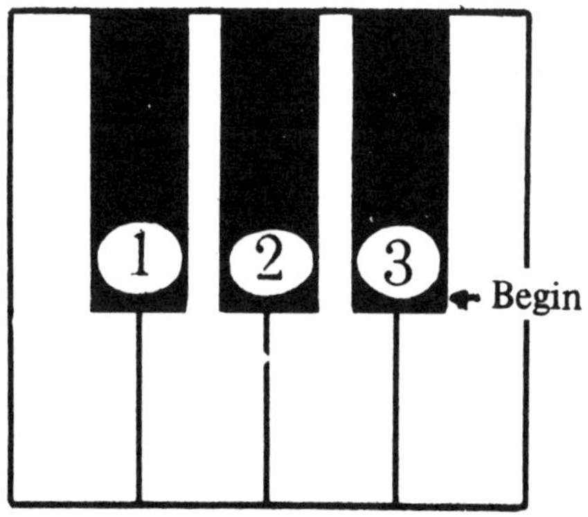

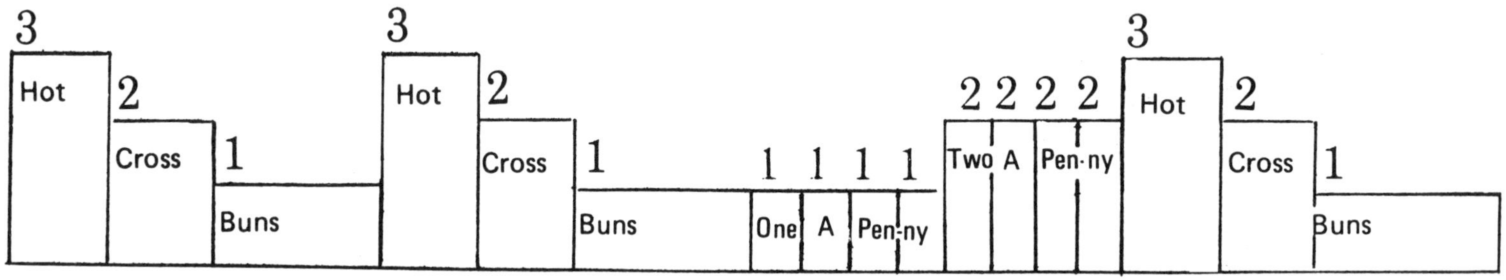

Left Hand

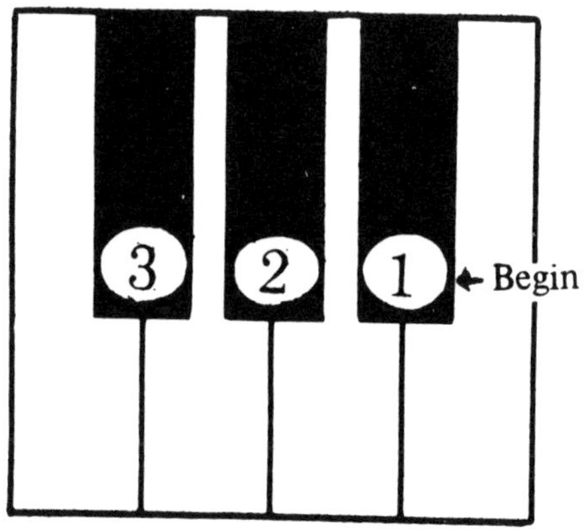

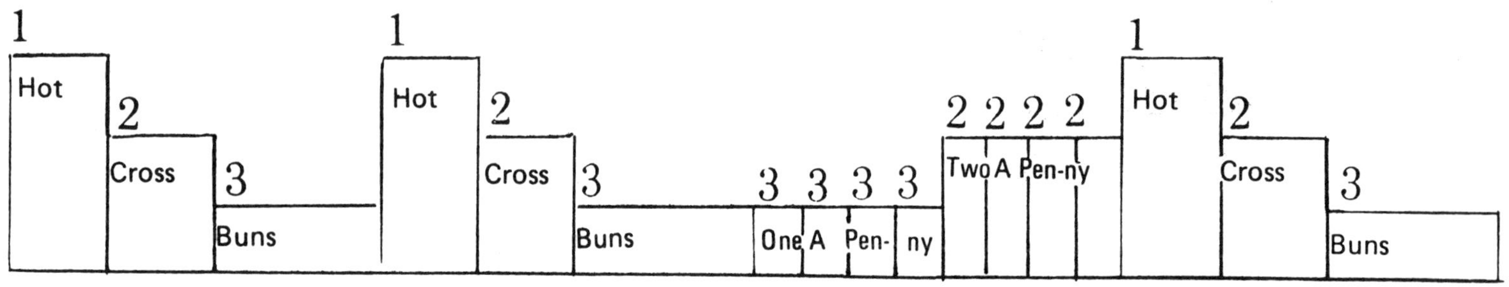

Transpose to the three white keys just to the left of the triplets.

Find the patterns that step down. How many are there? Where do the notes repeat 4 times?

Right Hand

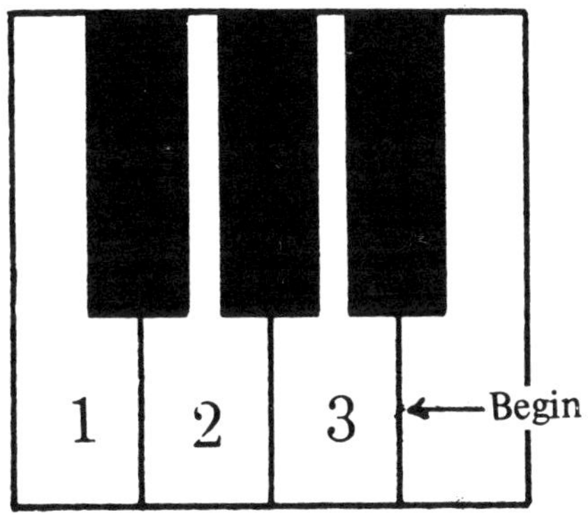

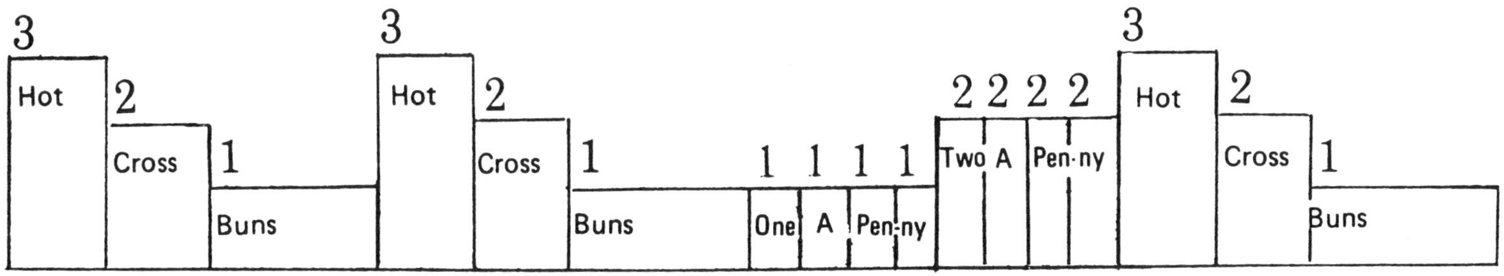

Left Hand

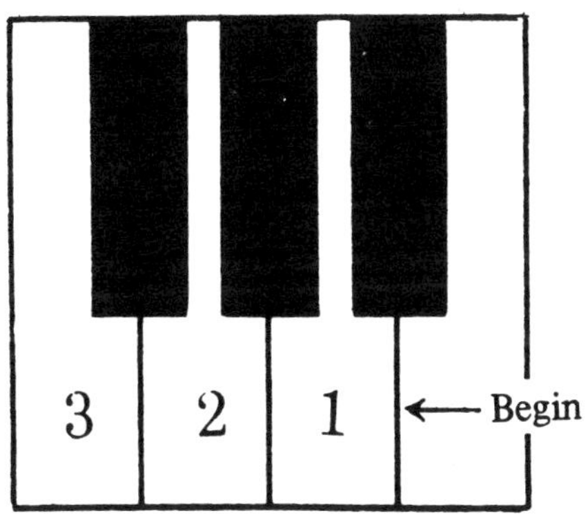

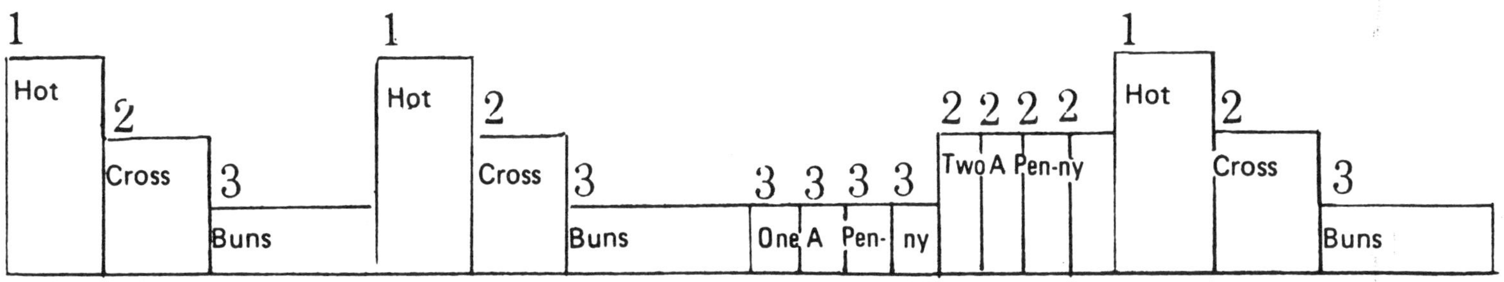

BUGLE CALL

Notice that this melody jumps from a lower note to a higher note. This is called a "skip". It first skips up, then it skips down.

1. Sing and shape.
2. Sing and clap.
3. Sing and play in the air.
4. Sing and play on the piano.

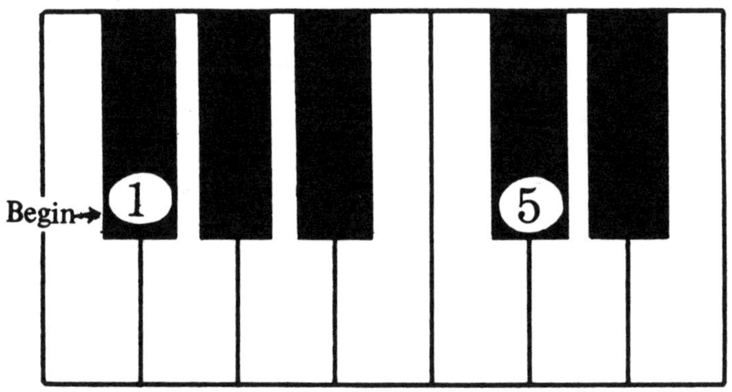

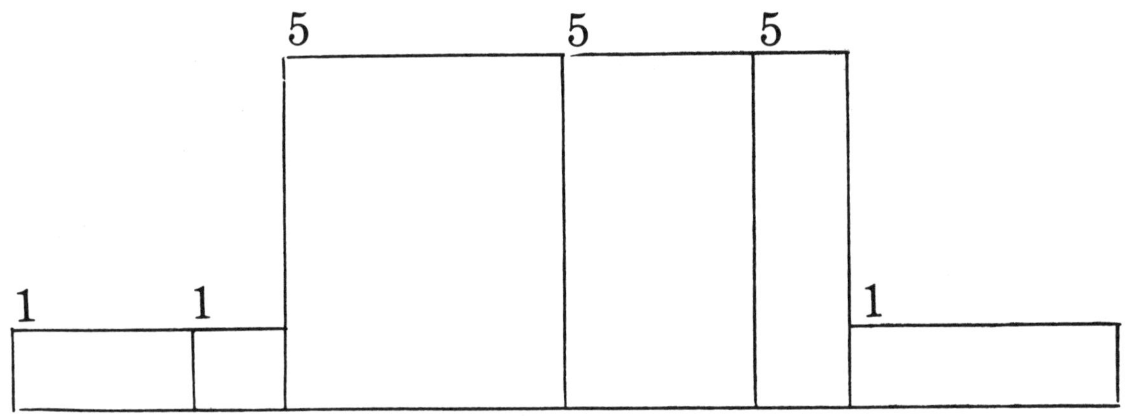

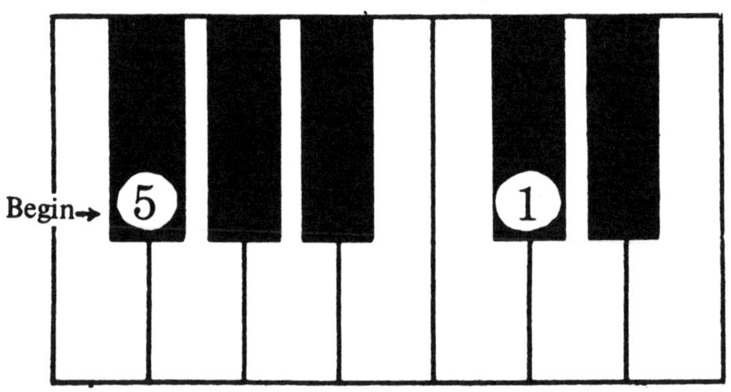

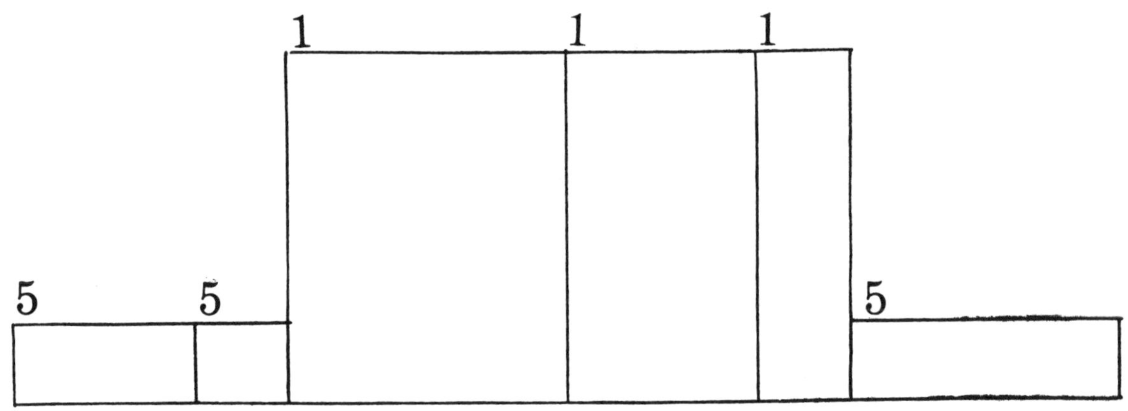

BUGLE CALL

Transpose as shown on these keyboards. Also play it high and low on your piano. See how many different places you can play this.

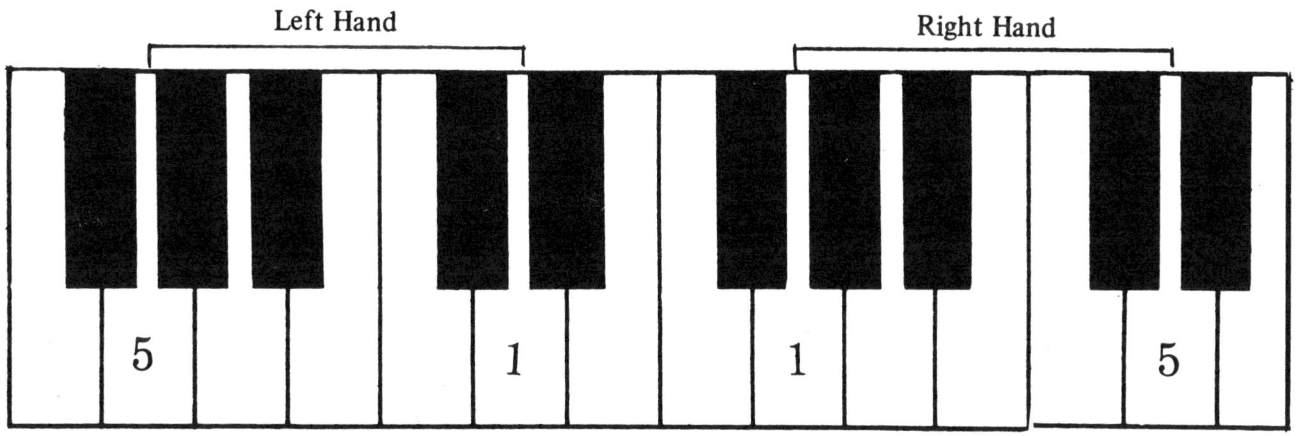

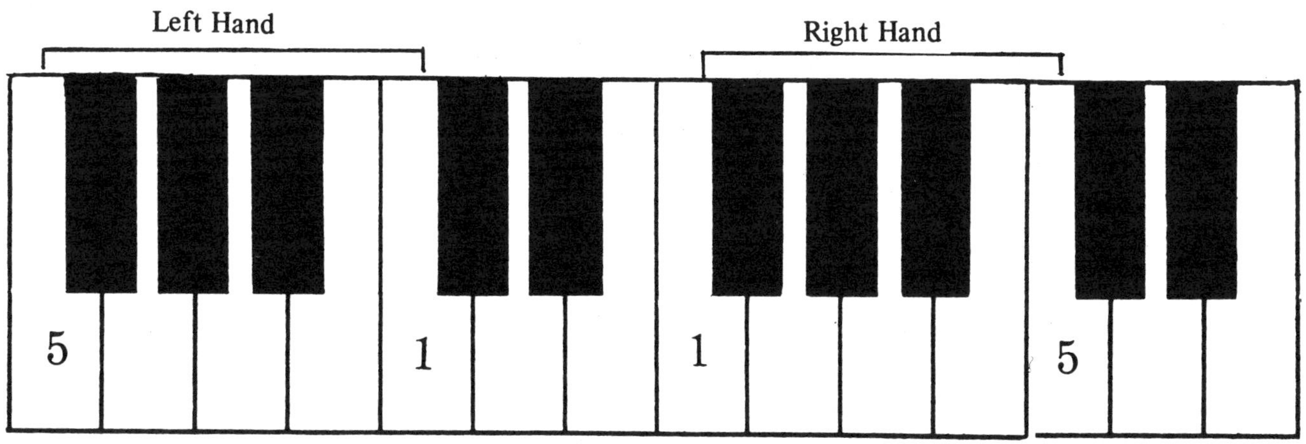

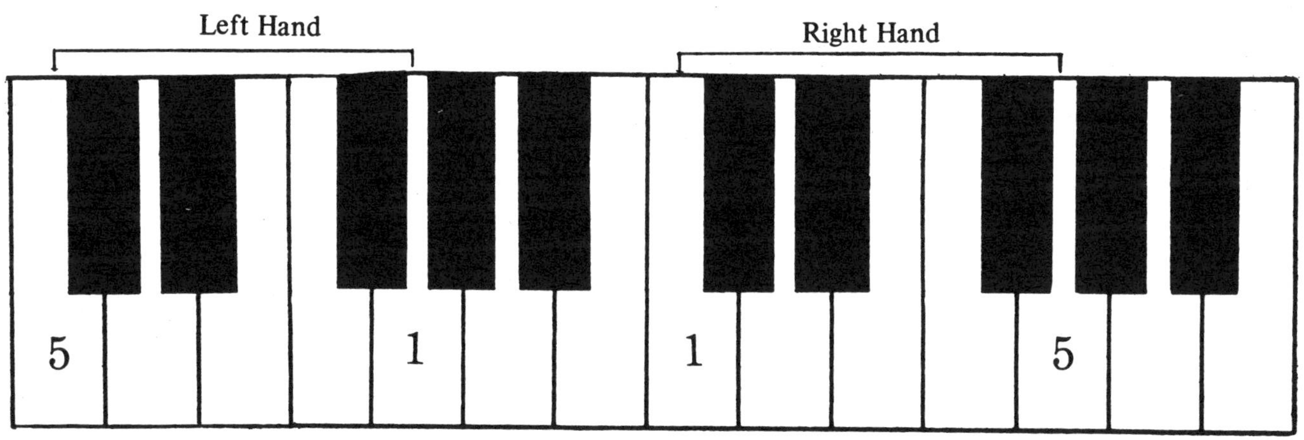

UP AND DOWN

Here we use all five fingers as we step up and step down.
First go up the hill with the right hand, then without stopping go down the hill with the left hand.

1. Sing and shape the melody up the hill with the right hand - then down the hill with the left hand.
2. Sing and clap the melody.
3. Sing and play the melody up the hill with the right hand - then down the hill with the left hand.
4. Sing and play the melody on the piano using right hand - then left hand.

Right Hand

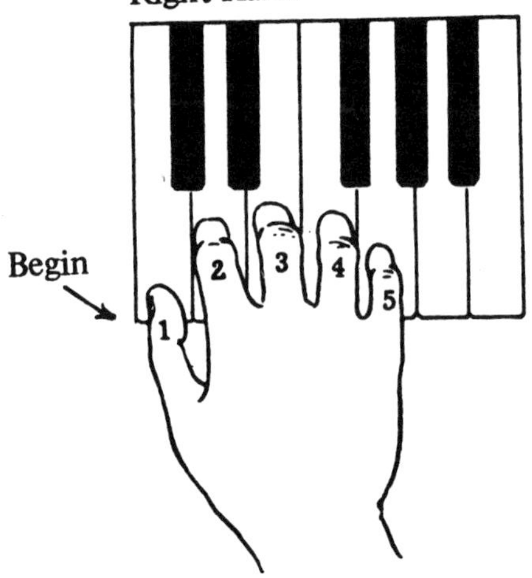

1	2	3	4	5	5	5
STEP-	PING,	STEP-	PING	UP	THE	HILL

Left Hand

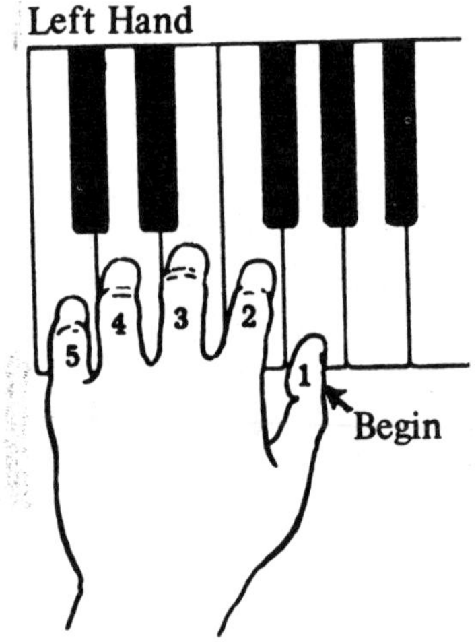

1	2	3	4	5	5	5
STEP-	PING	DOWN	AND	HOME	WE	GO

UP AND DOWN

Transpose "Up and Down" as shown here. Just remember to move each finger up to the next closest key.
Play these high and low.

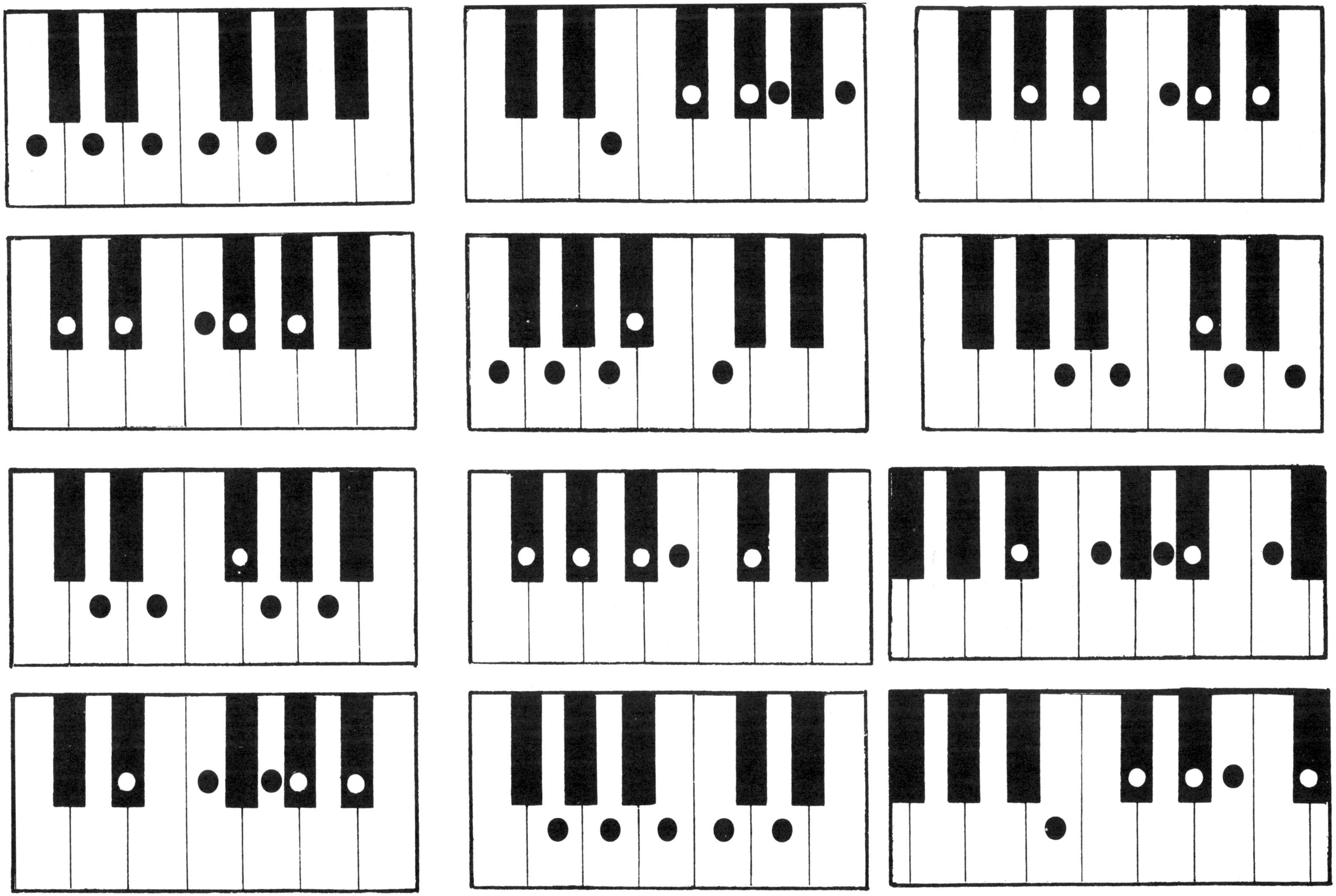

SKIPPING

Notice that "Skipping" uses every other finger.

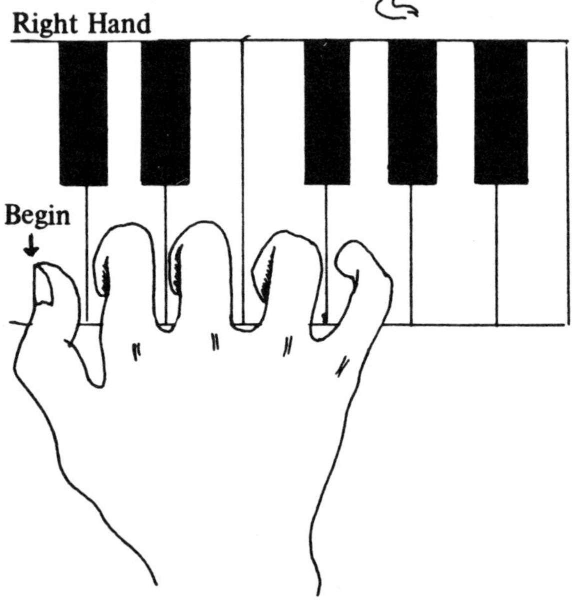

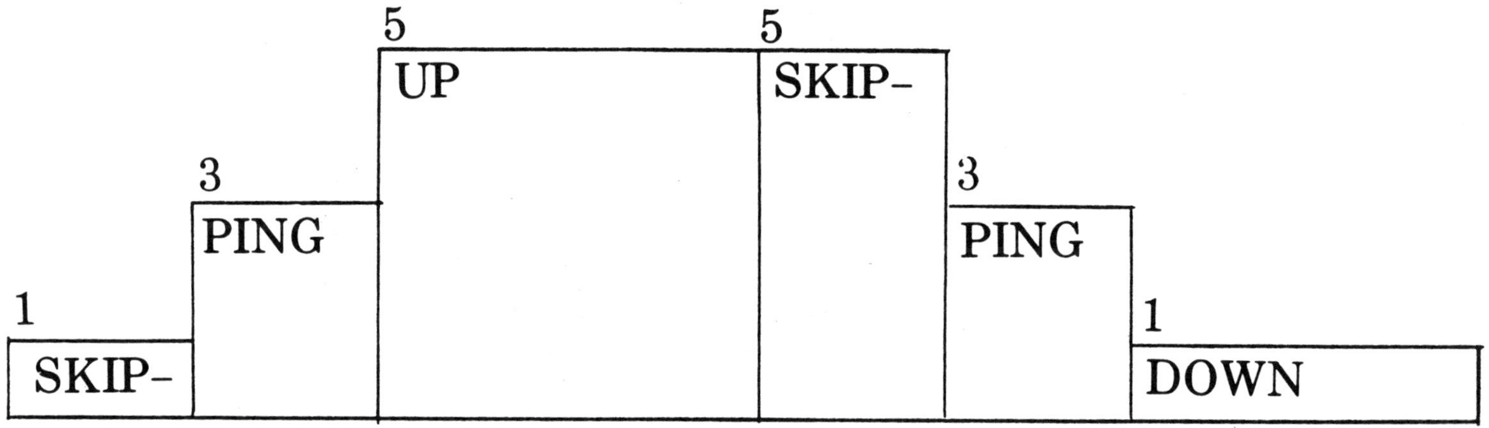

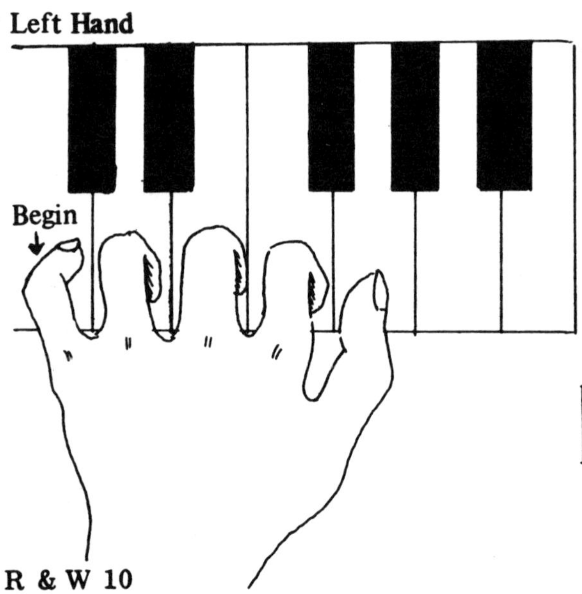

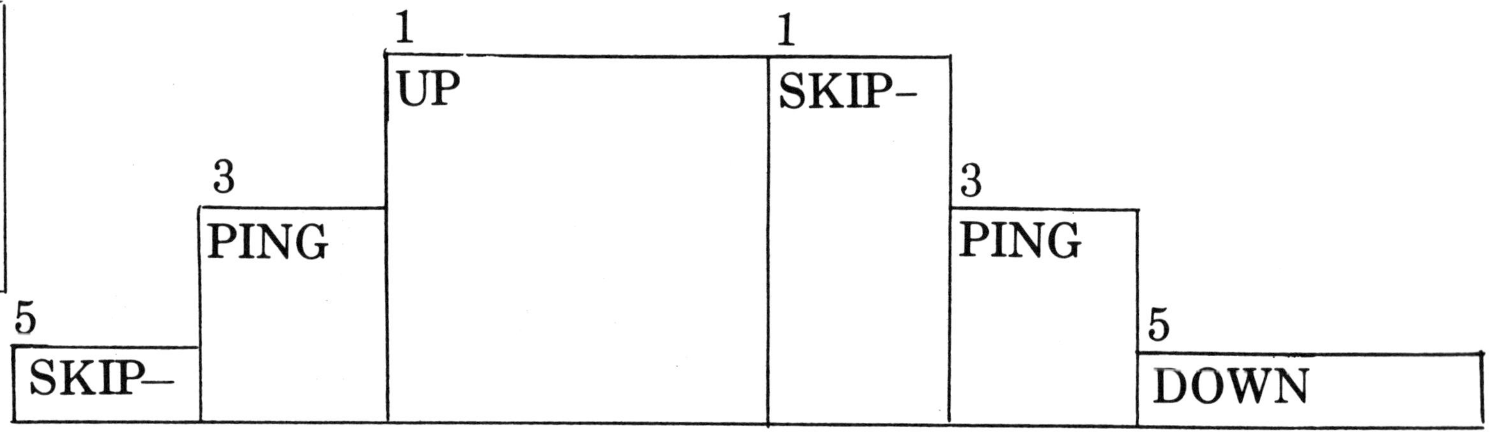

SKIPPING

First play "Up and Down" (all five tones), then immediately play "Skipping (three tones) for each keyboard.

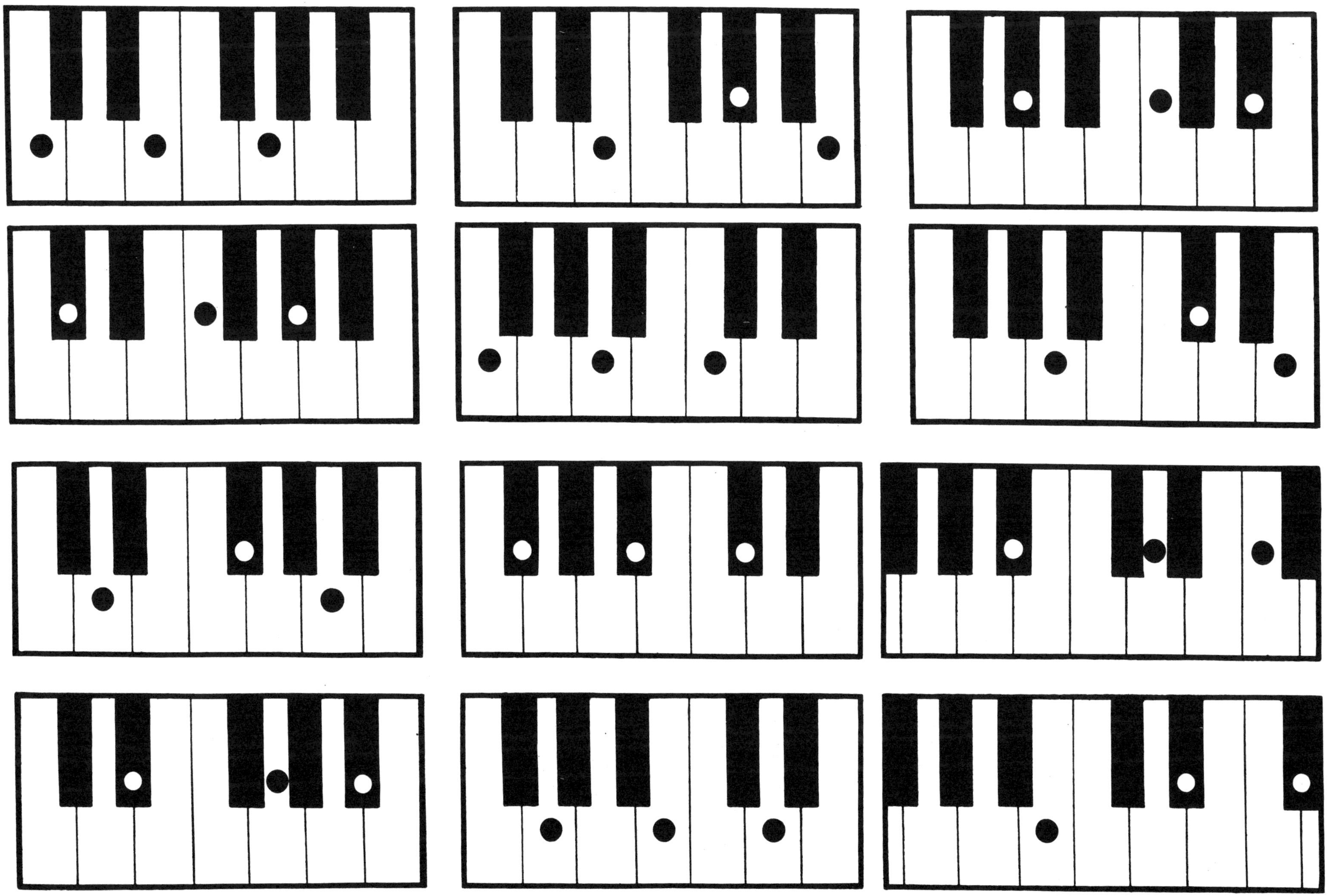

Play the first note with your left hand, then play the rest of the melody with your right hand. Look at the music, not at your hand.

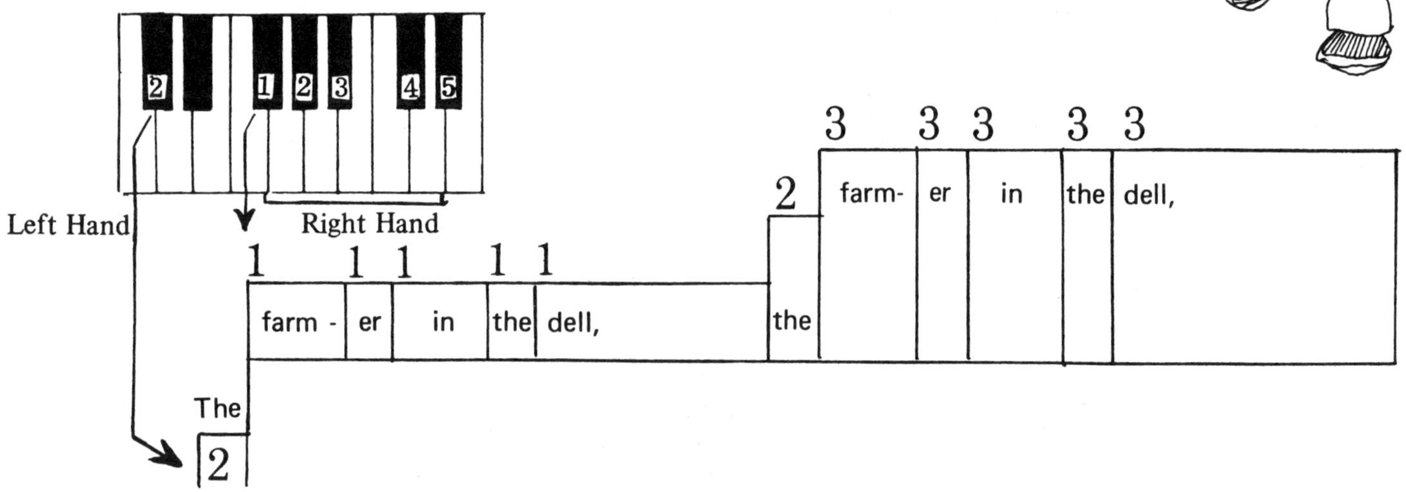

Find a partner and play this again as a duet.
Take turns playing the melody and the accompaniment.

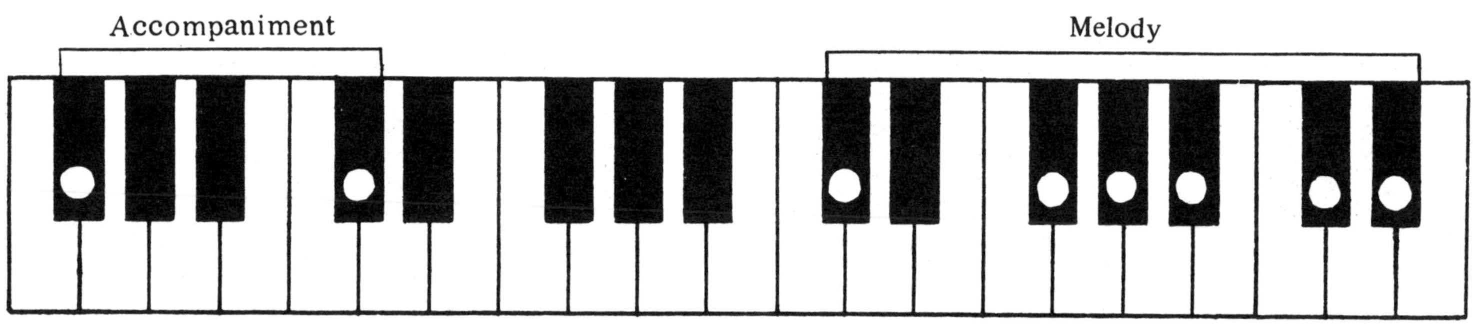

THE FARMER IN THE DELL

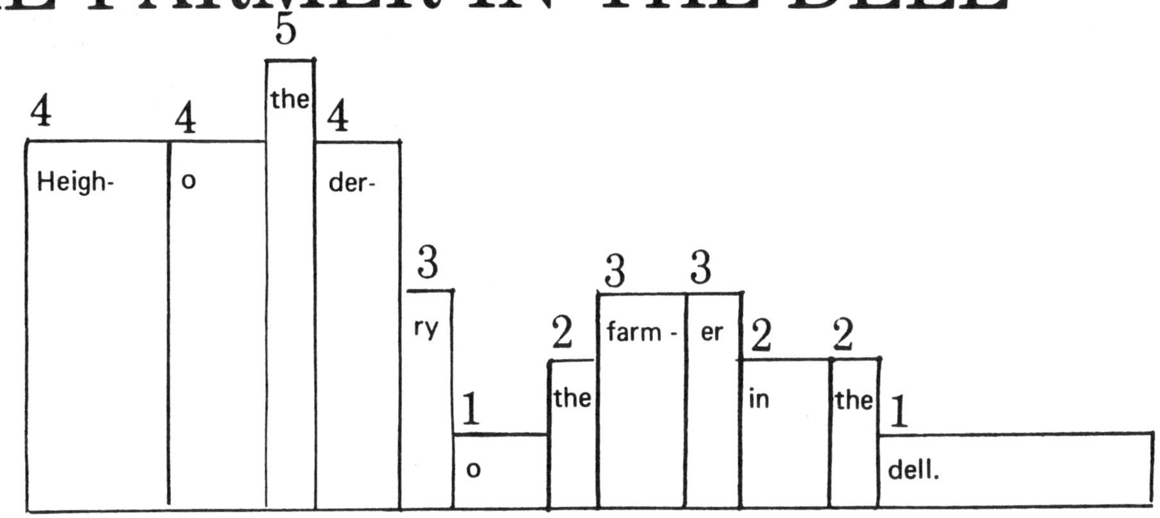

Transpose as shown on the keyboard.

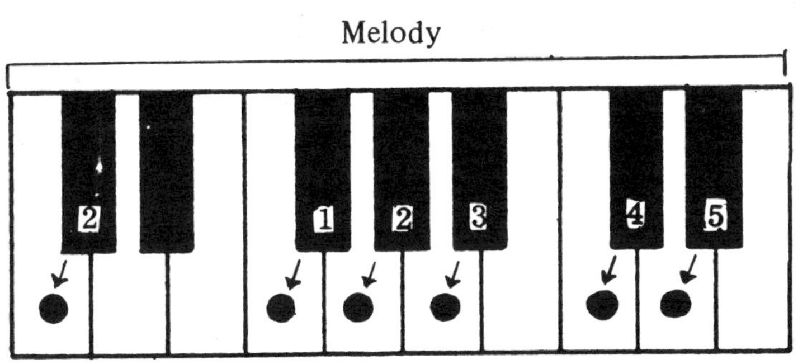

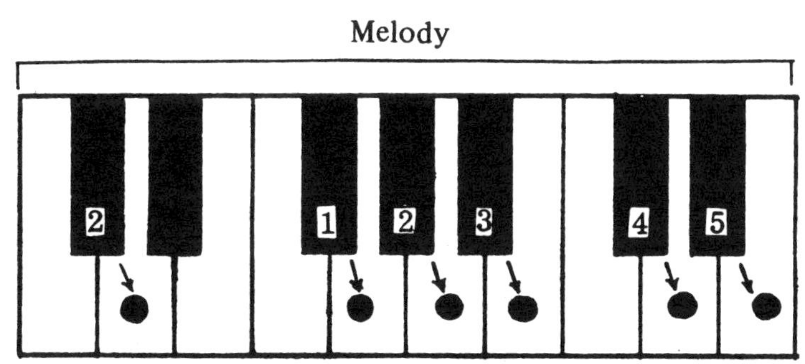

Steps and Skips

This melody moves by steps and skips.
Notice its shape.
Play first the right hand,
then the left hand.

Right Hand

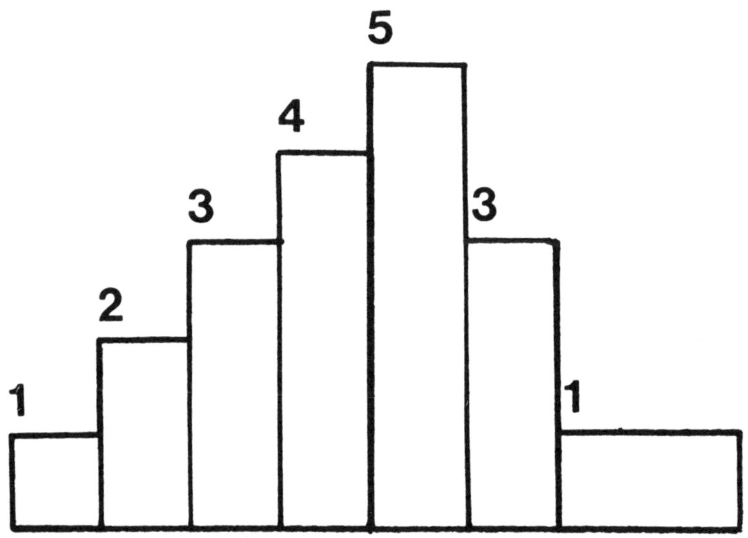

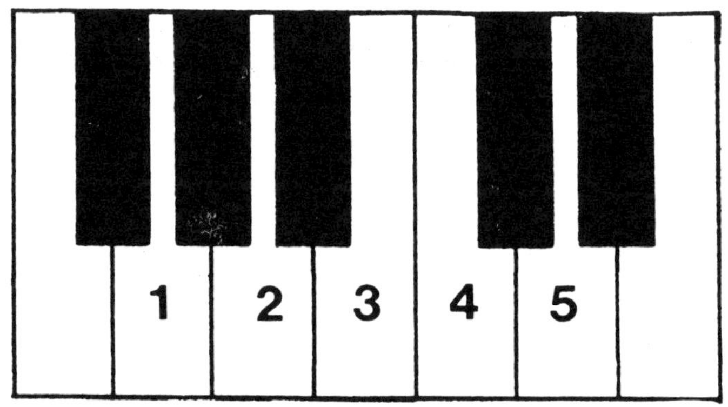

Left Hand

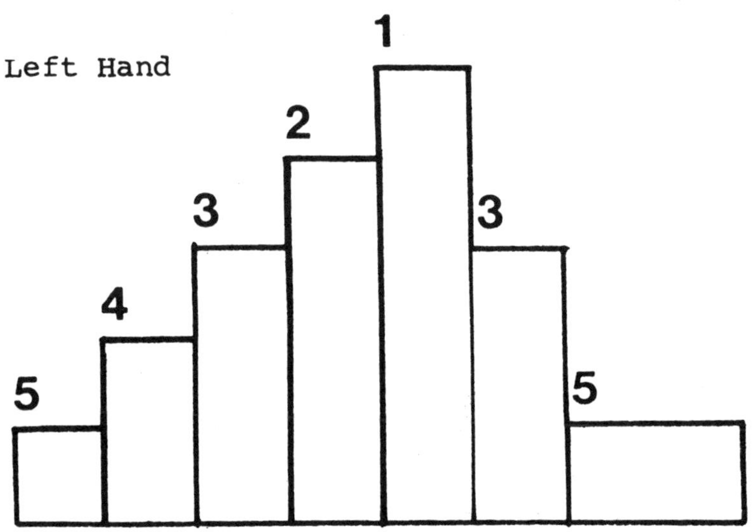

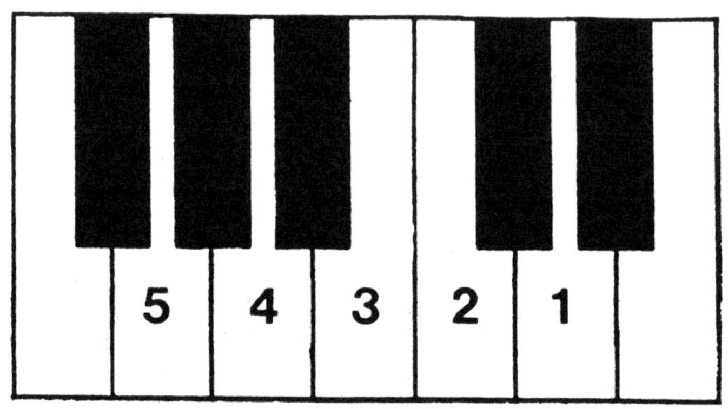

THE MUSICAL ALPHABET

The piano keyboard uses the seven letters of the alphabet from A to G. Remember where the letters are in relation to the triplets and twins.

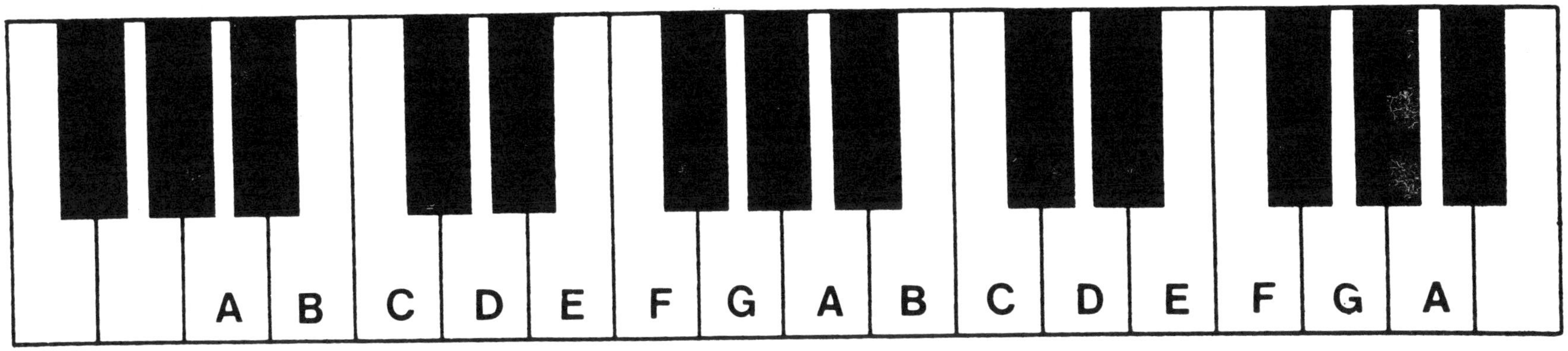

Fill in the A, B, C's on this keyboard.

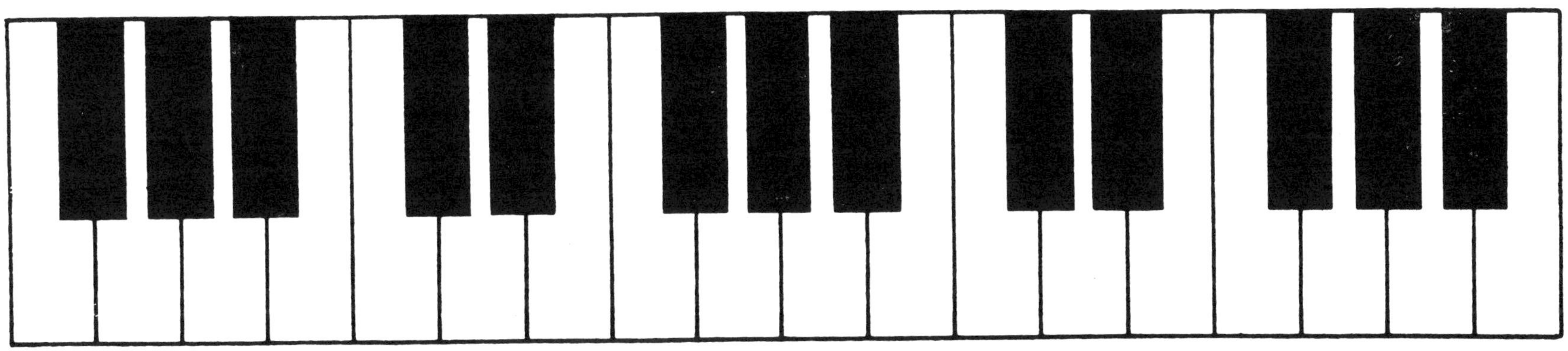

THE GRAND STAFF

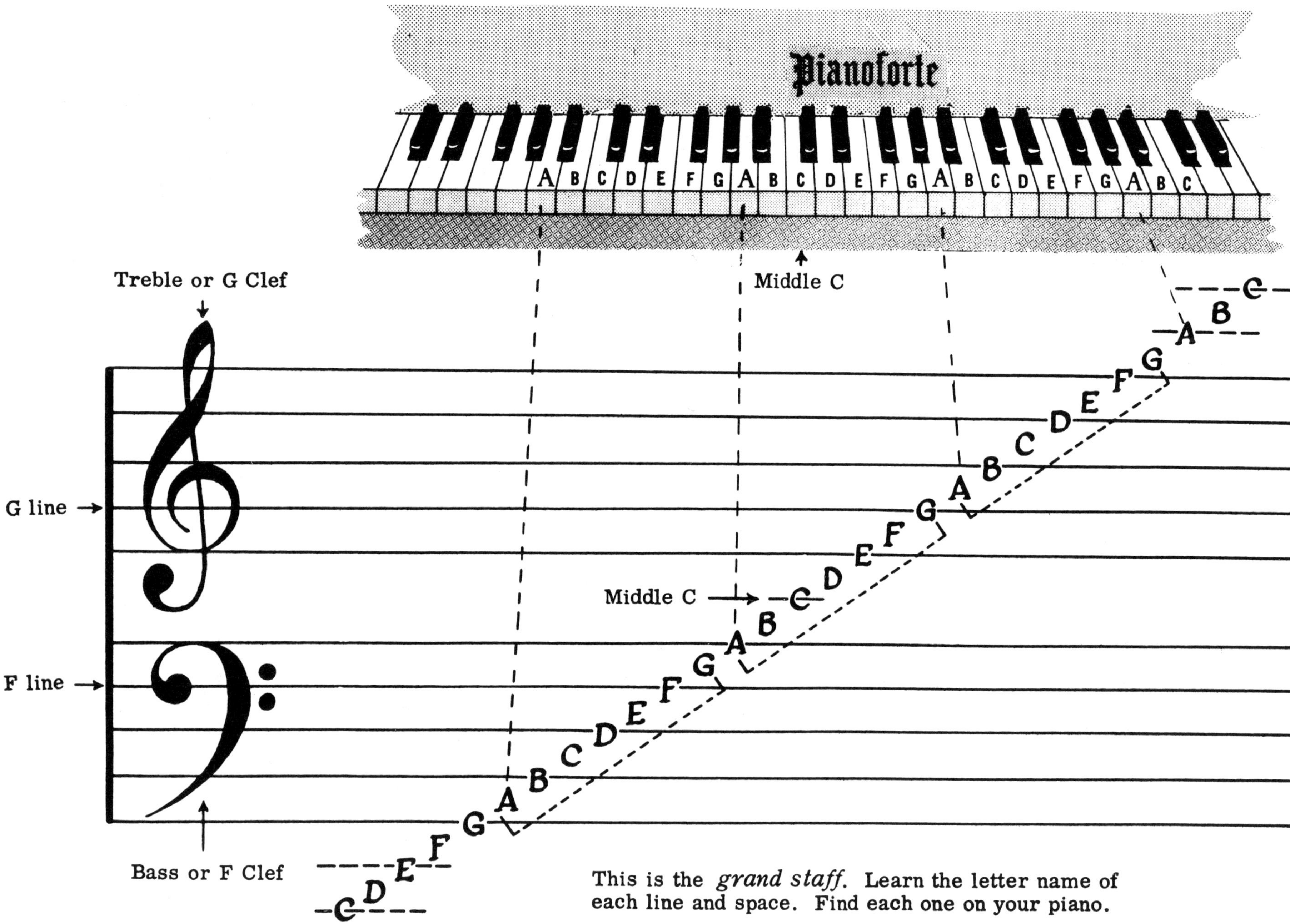

This is the *grand staff*. Learn the letter name of each line and space. Find each one on your piano.

GRAND STAFF FILL—IN

Study page 18, then write the letter name of each line and space on this page.

SHARPS

Move up to the very next key to find the SHARP. Notice that two of the sharps are white keys.

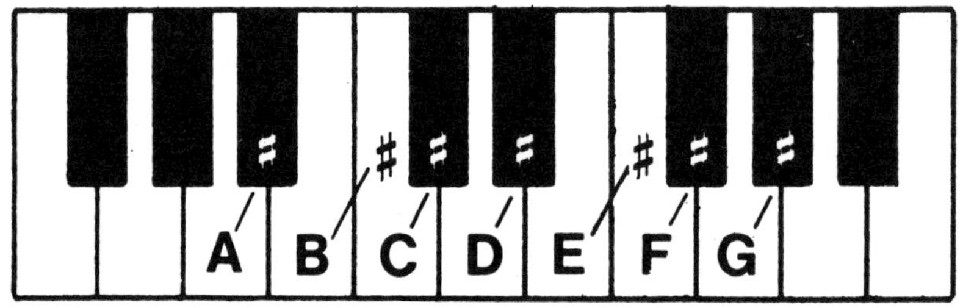

SHARP KEY SIGNATURES

To name sharp key signatures, look at the last sharp and count up one letter to the keynote. The key of C major has no sharps or flats.

6 sharps F# 5 sharps B 4 sharps E 3 sharps A 2 sharps D 1 sharp G

Here is "STEPPING" in the key of E major. E is the *keynote*.

FLATS

Move down to the very next key to find a FLAT. Notice that two of the flats are white keys.

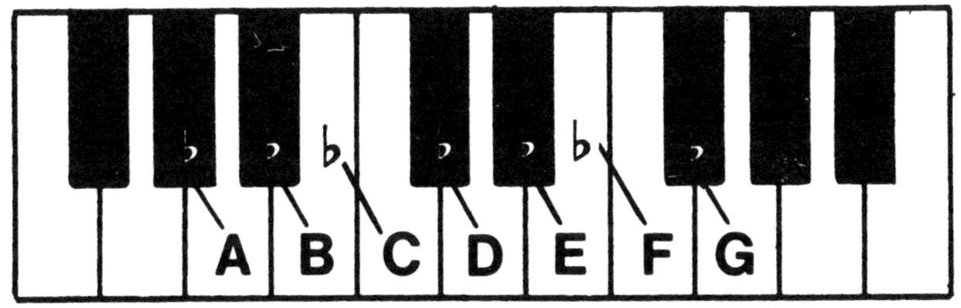

FLAT KEY SIGNATURES

To name flat key signatures, find the next to last flat which will be the keynote. Remember that the key of F major has one flat.

6 flats G♭   5 flats D♭   4 flats A♭   3 flats E♭   2 flats B♭   1 flat F

Here is "STEPPING" in the key of E♭ major. E♭ is the *keynote*.

R & W 19

MUSICAL NOTATION

TIME SIGNATURES

Some notes are longer than others. In "Stepping Up", there are quarter notes (one count) and half notes (two counts).

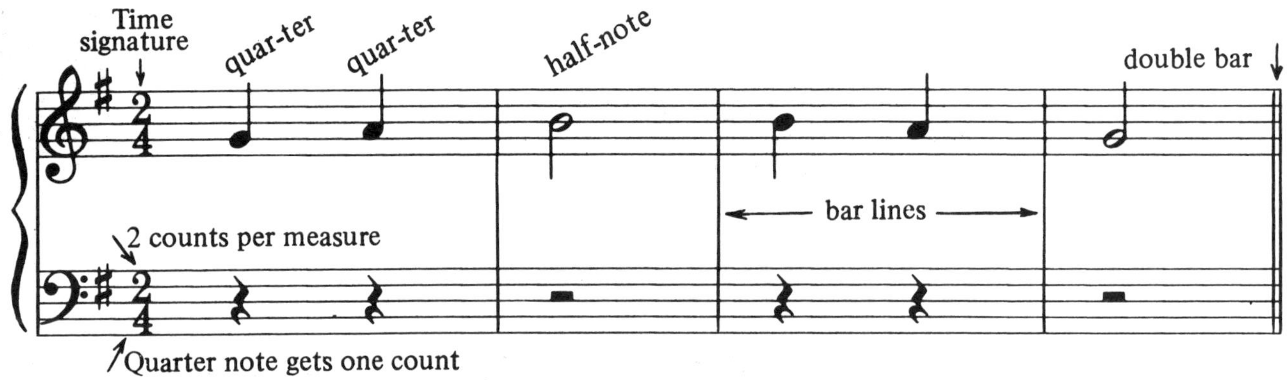

A quarter note or a quarter rest  gets one count 

A half note or a half rest  gets two counts 

A dotted half note or a dotted half rest  gets three counts 

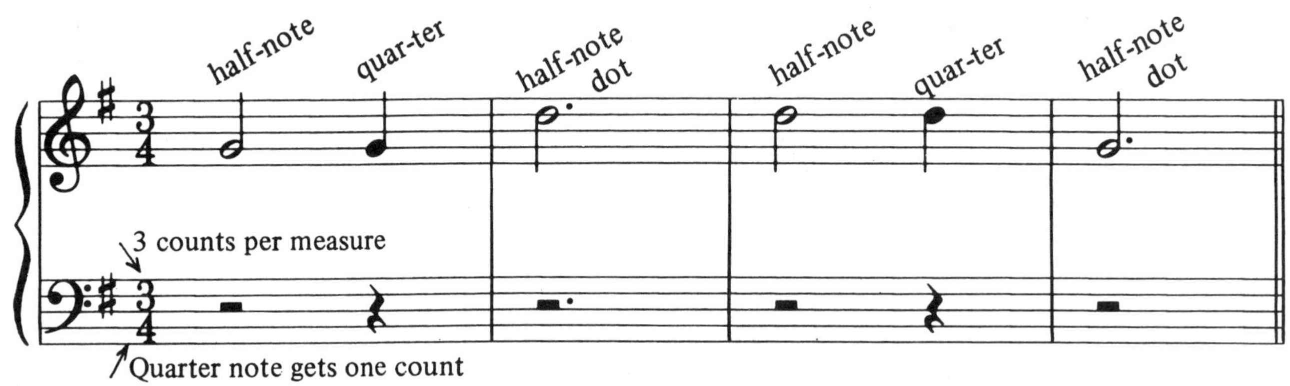

HOT CROSS BUNS

In "Hot Cross Buns" we use quarter notes, half notes and whole notes.

A whole note or a whole rest gets four counts

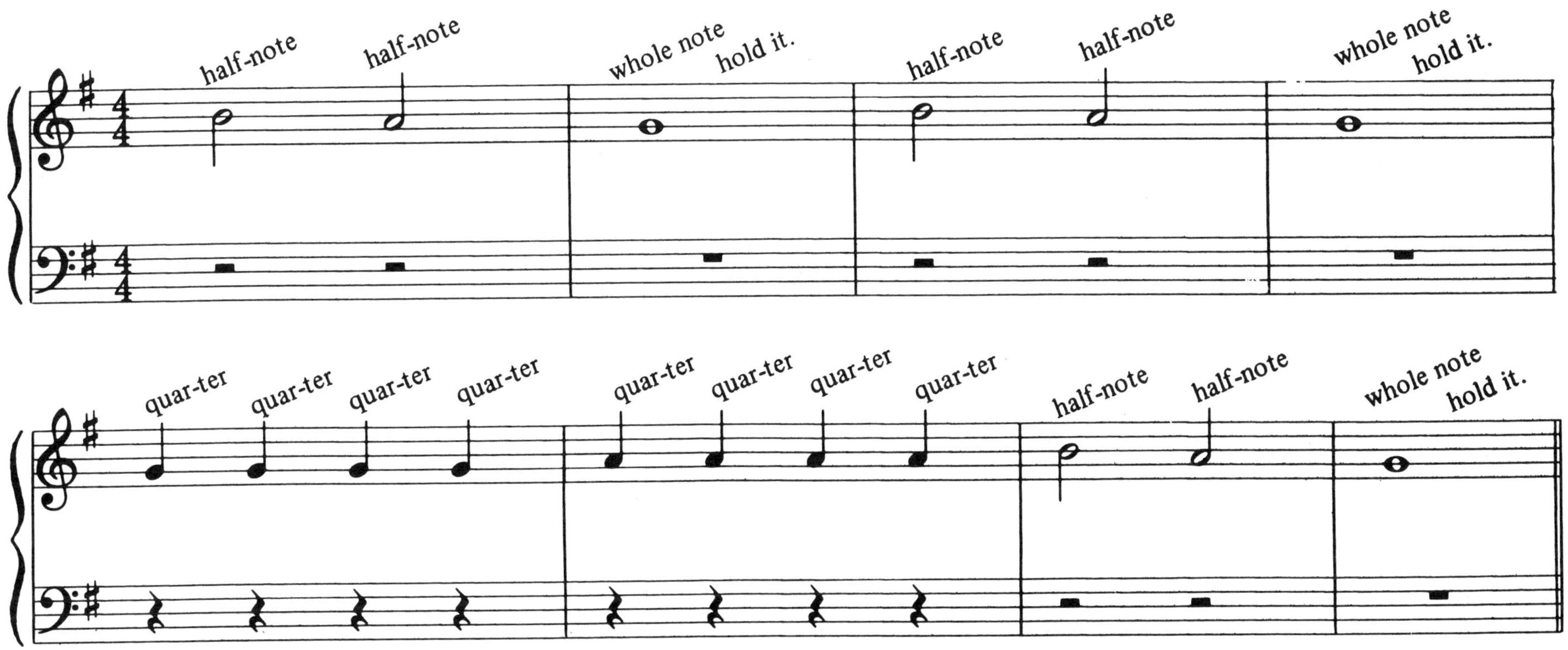

LEGATO STUDY

Let the weight of your arm shift from one finger to the next.
Make a slow circular motion with your wrist as you play from the bottom note to the top and back to the bottom.
Here we learn that two eighth notes get the same time as one quarter.

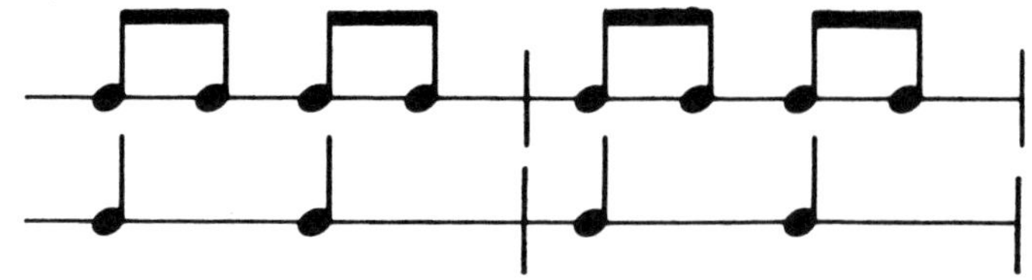

Right Hand

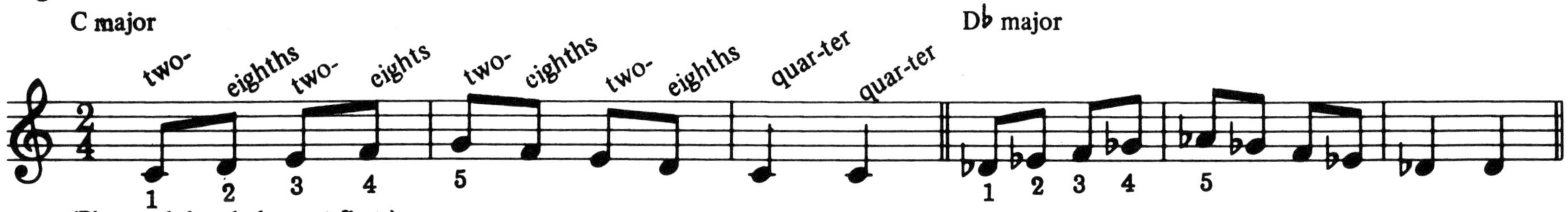

(Play each hand alone at first)

Left Hand

LEGATO STUDY

Now transpose this to play in A♭, A, B♭ and B major.

MARY HAD A LITTLE LAMB

Here we have a song with a dotted quarter and eighth note rhythm. A good way to count this is:

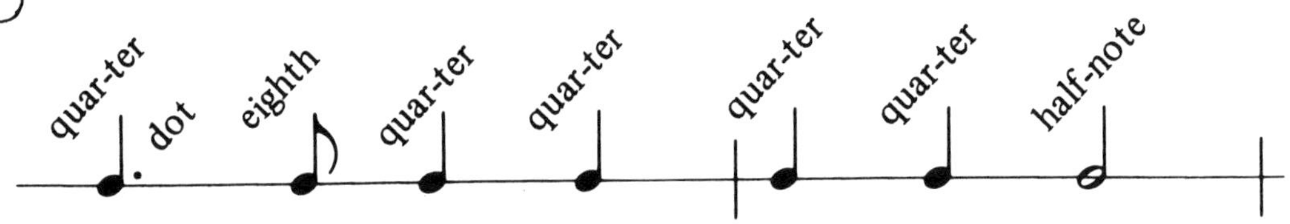

(Right hand)

(Left hand)

VARIATION

This *variation* of "Mary Had A Little Lamb" uses the same rhythm but changes the direction of the melody. Play this, then see how many variations you can make up.

Transpose to E and A major

R & W 25 & 26

OLD WOMAN

First, tune up in the key of D major. Leave your fingers on those keys and begin this melody on the top note.

Observe the dynamic markings here.

f = forte (loud)

p = piano (soft)

Transpose to D♭ and E♭ major
R & W 27 & 28

OLD WOMAN
Variation

In this variation of "Old Woman" the rhythm is the same but the melody is "up-side down" with the exception of one measure. Can you find it?

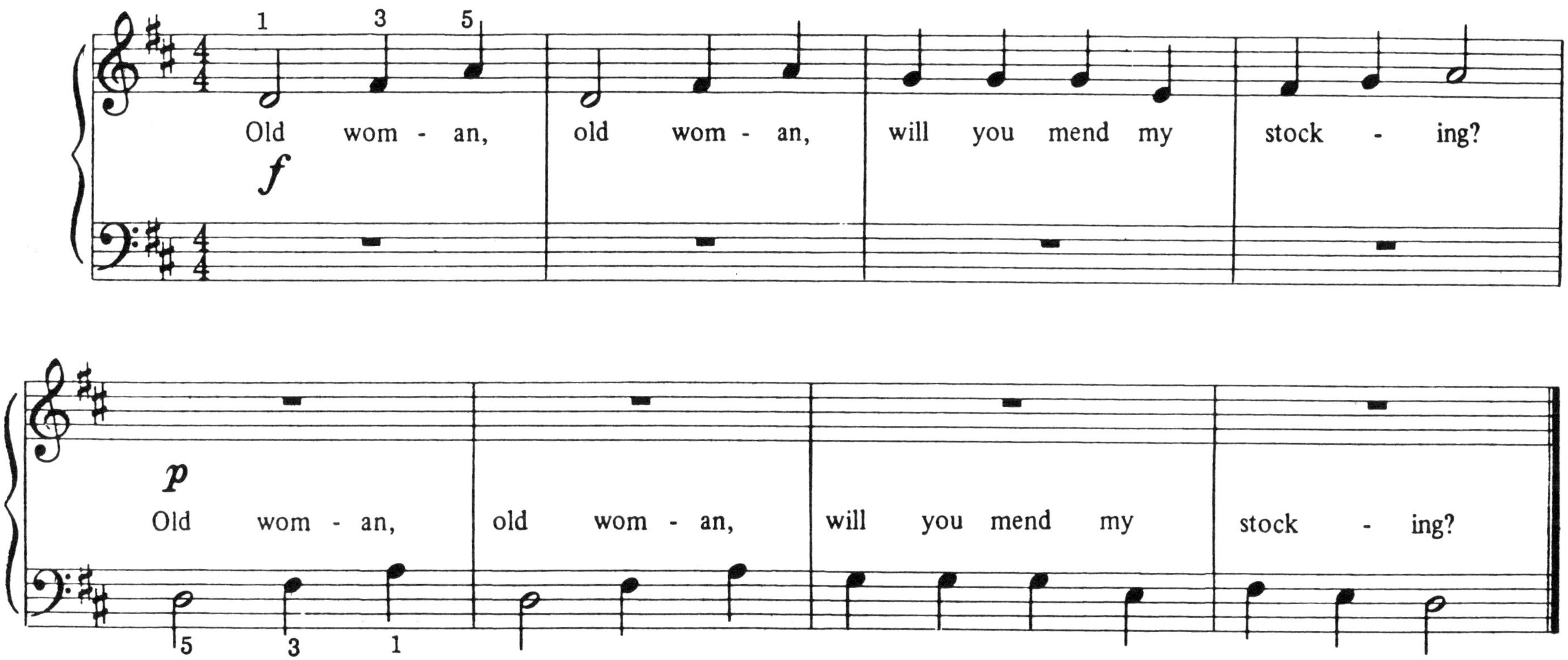

Transpose to E and C major

1214

Here there are six counts per measure and the eighth note gets one count – but count this way:

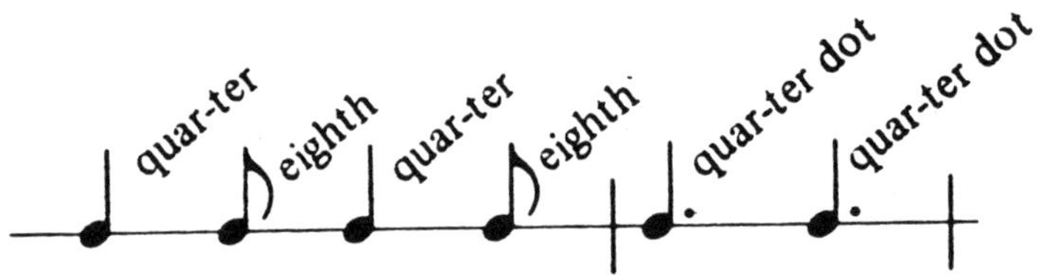

SWEETLY SINGS

Also, notice the "tied" notes (♩. ‿ ♩.). Play the first one and just hold the second one. (Don't play it again.)

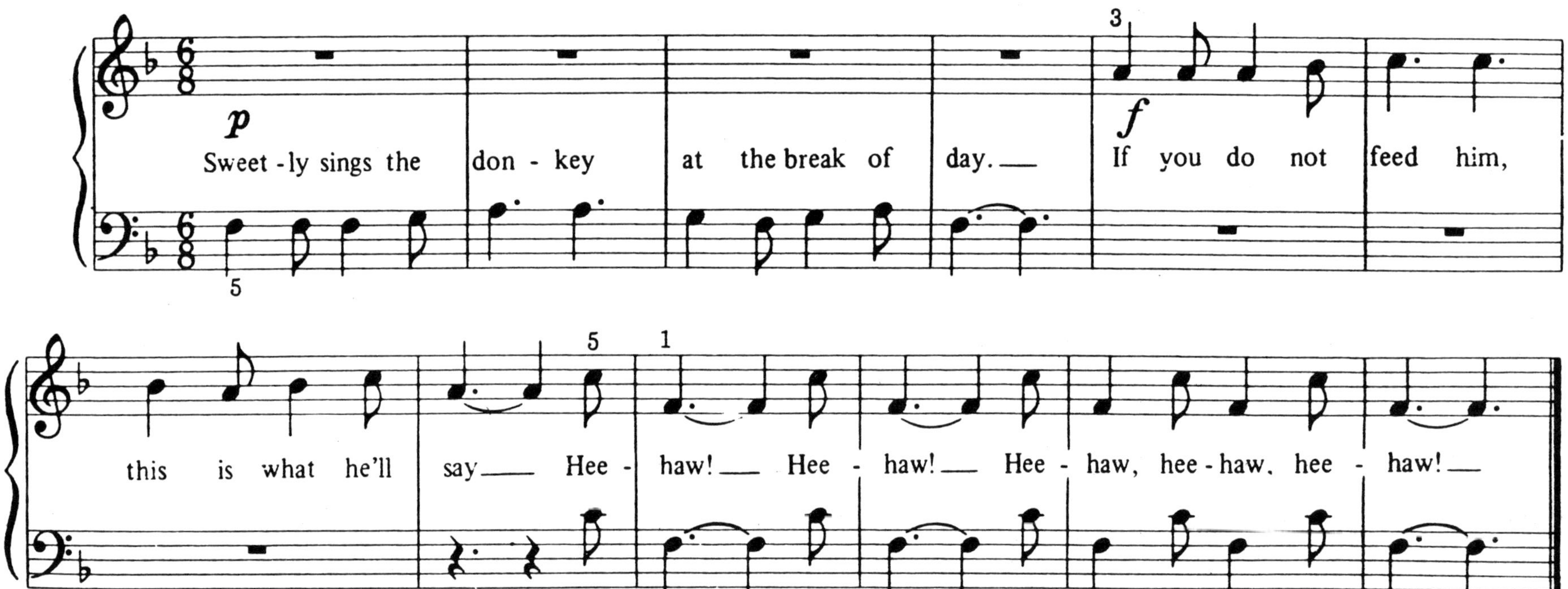

Transpose to E and G major

1214

THE DONKEY

After playing this variation of "Sweetly Sings the Donkey," make up other variations that use skips, steps and repeated tones. Also observe the dynamics.

(crescendo sign)	crescendo	getting louder
(diminuendo sign)	diminuendo	getting softer

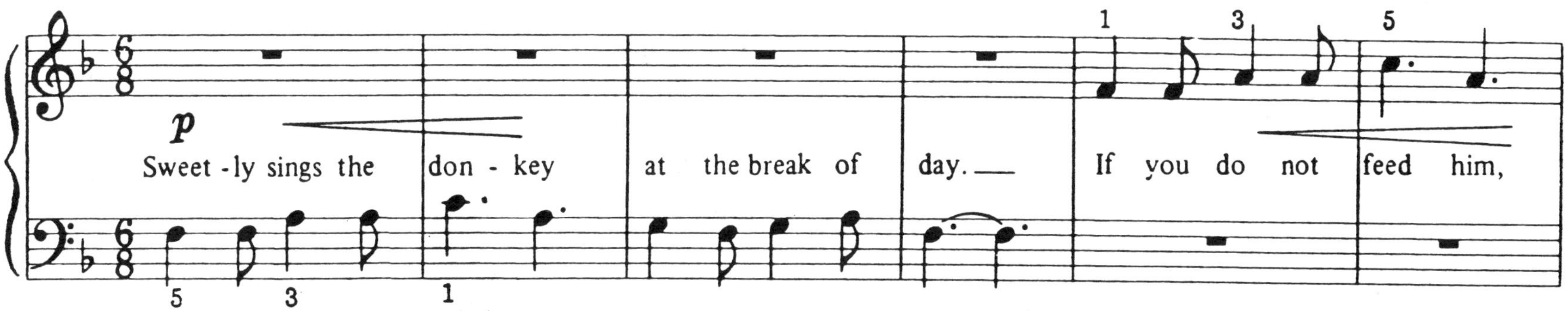

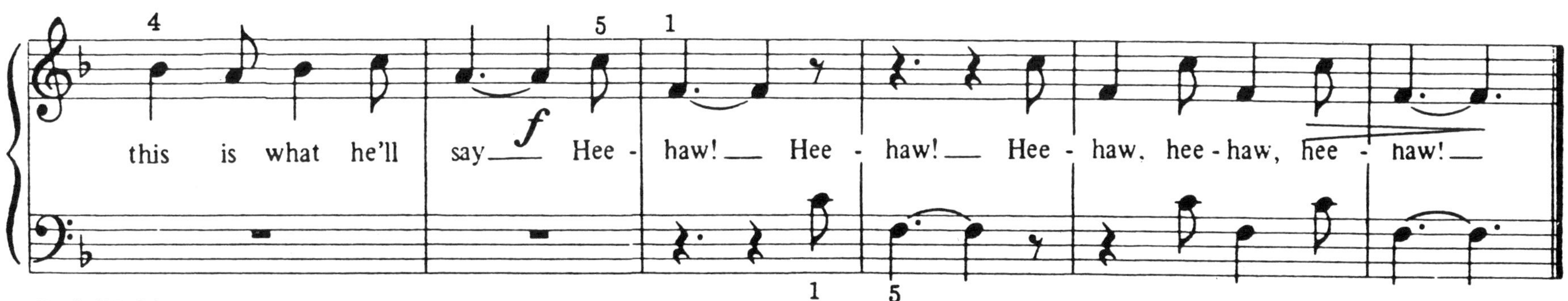

1214